Hollie loves writing poetry. She started her diary in rhyme when she was 6 years old. After another 19 years, she dragged her brother to Poetry Unplugged in London's Poetry Café and read a poem; the first time she had read to anyone other than her mum or partner. Since then, she has been reading her poetry around the UK and beyond, from Latvia to Poland, Morocco and Australia. With her album *Versus*, she became the first poet ever to record and perform at Abbey Road Studios in London.

Hollie has garnered titles such as *Boundary Breaker* (Marie Claire), *Internet Sensation* (Best Daily), *Incredible* (Huffington Post). Benjamin Zephaniah said, *I can't take my ears off her*. In 2015, she won the Arts Foundation Fellowship in Spoken Word.

Hollie has performed in a lot of places but has had a few favourite spots to read and hear live poetry: Bang Said The Gun (London), Neu Reekie (Edinburgh), Wandering Word Stage (Shambala Festival), Cathedral Quarter Arts Festival (Belfast), The Poetry Stage (Latitude Festival), Loud Poets (Edinburgh / Glasgow), Word Life / Off The Shelf (Sheffield), Freeway Poets (Bournemouth), Ledbury Poetry Festival, Humbermouth Festival (Hull), Hammer and Tongue (various locations), Lingo (Dublin), Chill Pill (London), Cuirt International Festival of Literature (Galway) and the Festival Internacional de Poesía (Medellín, Colombia).

Hollie is from a village near Reading. Her parents are both from Glasgow. Her favourite poems are probably Barry McGuire's *Eve of Destruction*, *Please Mrs Butler* by Janet and Allan Ahlberg and anything Maya Angelou ever wrote or said.

www.holliepoetry.com
@holliepoetry
facebook.com/holliepoetry

Other titles by Hollie Poetry
Versus – A Double Album of Spoken Poetry (2014)
Nobody Told Me – Poems on Parenthood (Blackfriars Books 2016)

My Gran used to call me
Cherry Pie
when I was a baby

Cherry pie is one
of the first memories
I have of my grandad

When I was a teenager I worked
in Little Chef
motorway services
microwaving
frozen bags
of
pre-made
cherries
in syrup

I have a long relationship with cherries

for Gaga and Papa
Gran and Grandad

Burning Eye

This edition published by Burning Eye Books 2015

www.burningeye.co.uk

@burningeyebooks

Burning Eye Books
15 West Hill, Portishead, BS20 6LG

ISBN 978 1 90913 655 7

Cover design & sunset pages by Enrica Casentini
Black & white drawings not otherwise attributed are by Xueyun Feng

CHERRY PIE
by Hollie Poetry

Poems / *Illustrations*

BUNGALOWS AND BISCUIT TINS 8
Televisions – Xueyun Feng

CARE HOME 12

CAFE CULTURE 13
Grandma (top) – Jenna Thomspon
Grandma (lower) – Rebecca Riddle

CHERRY PIE 14
Cherry Pie – Dilara Arin

COCOA BUTTER 16

CLUBBING 17

CUPCAKES AND SCONES 18
Various sweets sketches – Xueyun Feng
Cupcake and Glasses – Sophie Wainwright

CV 26
CV comic – Rachel Smith

DEAR LONDON 27
Bus – Xueyun Feng
Blackberries and Rosehips – Ľubica Oslancová

EAT MY FIG: AN INTRODUCTION 33
Large fig – Sonya Smith
Whole fig – Rachel Blackwell
Small figs – Lydia Nowak

EAT MY FIG 34
Fig – Rebecca Riddle

HATE 36
Chairs – Xueyun Feng

HEADACHE 39
Sleeping girl – Emma Payne

HUMANS 40
Child & Penguin – Aurora Cacciapuoti

LEEK AND POTATO SOUP 42
Soup – Ana Granado

MARKS OUT OF TEN 44
People – Kate Alizadeh

MATHEMATICS 46
People – Emma Conway

MOON 48
Girl & the Moon – Catrin Welz Stein

OCEAN FLOOR 49
Boat – Ana Granado

PINK 54
Z the Zebra Rider – Dilara Arin

PLAYING LACROSSE AT CAMBRIDGE UNIVERSITY 56

REVERSE 58
Dancer – Enrica Casentini

SILENCE 63
Silence – Rachel Orme

SPIN 64

School children – Emma Conway
Picking flowers – Sally Milligan

TEN ENGLISH GENTLEMEN 69
TRex Men – Fab Funky

TINKERBELL 72
Little Tink – Polly Crosby
Mechanic – David Evans

TOUCH 76
Strawberries – Xueyun Feng

VOICE 81
Wee lassie – Aurora Cacciapuoti

BUNGALOWS AND BISCUIT TINS

my grandmas are officially old now
94 and 86
they tell me war was not romantic
not a bit
don't believe those posters of the handsome soldiers
kissing loved ones who waited for them to come back
most endings were not like that
most loved ones died or loves burnt out
my grandmas go to more funerals
than parties now
neither of them like this

and they sit
observing everything

their christmases as kids were
sock stockings
a single bouncy ball
now i watch them watching
as great grandkids open hoards of presents
throwing half onto the floor

sometimes we row a bit
about what's right or wrong for 'us' to do
my pregnancy without a wedding ring
is something that we struggled through
talked it through
– agreed to disagree
and though i felt a little shamed
when she offered me her ring to wear
i knew she was just protecting me
from how people would've been to her
if she had done the same
the other took me to the side
my waist held tight in sympathy

loads of my generation
got knocked up too she whispered
we just kept it covered up
and married very quickly

i love it when they wink at me
telling secrets – drinking tea
i ask about their history
they know a lot of things – my grans

they sit
and watch it all

articulate, intelligent
kind and bossy, shy sometimes
as clocks tick time with icing topped – i watch
people stop to ask them if they want
another cup of tea
ten thousand and eighty three i've had
she looks to me
they all taste just the bloody same
says *i'm bored of my friends dying*

and people are so patronising
bending over – speaking shyly
slowly and politely – over-smiling
like my grandmas are both kids
telling me *leave nan she's just nattering for the sake of it*
calling their conversations gossip
like older people are all the same
ignoring everything they thought
before their brown hairs turned to silver grey
if you ever call it lilac rinse
i will slap your little face
says she wishes she could dance again
but i see her dancing all the time
and i love the fact me and my mum's mum
tell dirty jokes my mum won't like

we watch reruns of csi
the oldest says she's ripe to die
– younger siblings now all gone
funerals a daily song
the tea is sipped

my daughter loves the way they live
bungalows
and secret tins of biscuits
she nicks while my grandma sleeps
my youngest grandma does *chairobics*
for the over eighties
twice a week
and lives a larger life than most people my age
that I meet

i see life-lines run through both their faces
both of them my saving graces
i think our country's ageist
i wish more grandmas filled the pages
of our youth-obsessed tv screens

you teach us what real wisdom means

so though there's things we argue on
and your mindsets can be militant
and you always say i swear too much
i think you're fucking brilliant

//
When I first wrote this poem down, it was slightly different. Instead of 'shy sometimes', I had written 'sly sometimes'. After reading it out to my gaga, she said she was offended by the word 'sly'. She didn't want to be called sly. So I changed it, because I like her more than my poems. Even though she sometimes is sly. Especially when it comes to getting me to change my poems.

CARE HOME

she is treated like a queen here
breakfast at 9 – lunch at 1 – dinner at 6
the hairdresser comes 1 morning a week at 10am – *lovely young man*
a cup of tea in her room at 4 – *just hot water* – and a biscuit
aunt visits – freckled arms prop pillows and brighten each day
they check her twice in the night to make sure she's ok
– *that a'm no' deid!*

6 years until the letter - dad says
gran laughs – *bollocks to that – bugger the queen!*
clearly states this is her last christmas
hands out coins and chocolates
hidden in the top drawer by her bed bar
the great grandchildren chatter and laugh
out of sync with her hearing aid
apart from that
she's fine – *just tired* – she says – *and sore*

my train leaves at 3.34 tomorrow
queen street – waverley – kings cross
i wish i could be in scotland more
i wish i could be in scotland more
but the doors shut

gran says she wants to stop in less than 6 months
i don't want her to
but if she wishes
i hope that she does

CAFE CULTURE

i'd love to see my nans in soho
sitting in a café
as their lunch comes out
upon a piece of bark
i'd love to watch them give it back
and ask for a plate with that
i can just imagine how they'd do it
what a bloody cheek!
next we'll be replacing
our brass ornaments
with dirty driftwood out from sea

CHERRY PIE

when my mum sliced the cherry pie on the table
my granddad ran off and threw up
i'm so sorry dad
mum said
i'm so sorry
i forgot

i was nine years old then
no idea what had happened
but when my papa came back – he explained

two weeks of waiting on the shores of a war beach
as rowing boats came to collect them
and the only thing there for the soldiers to eat were
pre-packaged sweet syrup cherry tins

his mates were shot dead
the cherries were blood red
stench of rotting and sweet fruit
he was gagging with each breath
he said *war is a sham*
we had ice cream instead
he said *be kind not revengeful hollie*
don't believe all you read
and don't eat cherries in syrup
cos that stuff rots your dreams

COCOA BUTTER

Your lips are edibly soft today
you smell of pomegranate
and shake off the peals of laughter
as my friends see you moisturise
your thighs proudly
caked in cocoa butter
you smother my
almond avon cream
on your lips

THE OTHER BLOKES MUSCLE UP AGAINST IT
lipstick mate, lipstick

you couldn't give a shit
it feels good
when your lips don't crack

the beauty industry fights back
against you
doubling profits
with masculine packaging

grey and black stripes – straight
dark blood red
manly flavours like coffee or hemp
expertly designed containers
shaped like gun barrels
or bullet lead
important labels
to lessen the threat
of softer skin
like this
lip balm is
FOR MEN

CLUBBING

the poster said –
one in three reported rapes happen when the victim is drunk

a girl in the photo lies on the floor – young sweaty hair slapped across on her face good looking pretty – why? made up – why? upset – scared – sexy short skirt – bit of leg showing most of the time throwing up in clubs legless

it doesn't make me immediately angry
a standard protective family idea
i get it
when you're out and you're drunk it's less safe
don't get off your face – hollie

but on the back of the poster is the rest of the statistic –
if one third of all reported rape victims are over the limit
then two thirds are sober? wearing trousers
duffle coats buttoned to the collar – pyjamas – flat shoes
slippers – school uniforms – woolly grey tights
sitting in care homes and kitchens
dormitories and family rooms
with people they know

less posters of them
not sinful enough to be be pinned to a billboard perhaps
or too close to the bone
as if being – quiet – male – child – ugly – old – dry – ill – geeky – shy
is protection from this crime
                        – but it is power – violence and control
                        – not attraction and sex drive
the poster said
two in three reported rapes happen to a sober victim
i don't know about the offenders – the poster said nothing about them

CUPCAKES AND SCONES

still i see us
frost or snow
saturday nights
long socks
or stockings
jumpers and ties
badges and laces and rucksacks and lies
why is the adult school disco our most popular club night?

in england
this is a number one weekend retreat
lines of over eighteens
dressed like sexy thirteens
standing in school skirts
free entry allowed
if we dress like a
naughty school uniform crowd
i don't get it

i remember the warnings
gates closed at lunch
cos some pervert was stalking us
two of my friends had already been flashed
and as i walked home from school
i noticed the van
at the corner
up the road
a guy at the window
tongue between fingers
whistling blows
signing me blow jobs
as i stood in my school clothes
upping the pace
i sprint down the road
scared shitless

now thirteen years later
you want me to wear
the same uniform
– sexed –
to excite grown up stares

the school disco club night
we come in our hoards
get low with a school girl
without breaking laws
so i get chatted up by that dribbling man
who likes looking at me looking like i looked in year ten
i don't get it

i'd rather dance dressed like a woman
if i want to look sexy
i want to look like a woman
i'd rather be chatted up as a woman
and if perverts stare
well they should stare at a woman

because i like being a woman
i'm not a little girl
and years passing by
are not the end of the world
and my life as a woman is the best that it's been
and i like being me
i don't want to be thirteen again
worrying about school tests and perverts and spots
i don't want to wear school skirts or flirt in old pop-socks
as i'm told everyday to obsess to back to then
but i'd rather live life as a woman

still i see us
on saturday afternoons
sitting with friends in gorgeous new tea rooms
the cupcake is back
this is baking's new black

pastel shade icing and sprinkles on stacks
this new female fad is jamming up twitter
recipes sprinkling candies with glitter
i don't get it

i remember the parties
the last time i ate those
i was still using potties
grabbing at bowls of
soggy chip dippers
pineapple cheese sticks
and soft chocolate fingers
and in the middle of the table
making us sick
over-iced cupcakes with glittery bits

now twenty years later
this cupcake is back
as women sit nibbling
party girl snacks

i don't actually mind cupcakes
i'm just a bit tired
of every female fad
telling me i should still be a child
wrinkle cream anti-age
on all the shop aisles
now even our food is copying the style
jelly is back!
the cupcake is back!
beside topshop tills are these
lollipop stacks
big bowls of bubble gum
for daughters and mummies
next to pop-socks and cherries
why not nappies and dummies?
telling us that

fun is young
girly and sweet
quiet and coy
and thankful for treats
i don't want it

i'd rather eat food as a woman
if i want to meet friends
i want to meet as a woman
i'd rather drink afternoon tea as a woman
laugh and be happy and free as a woman

because i like being a woman
it's not a dirty word
and years passing by
are not the end of the world
and my life as a woman
so far
is the best that it's been
and i like being me
i don't want to be three again
with cakes held before me as bribes to be good
fingers grabbing at soggy-licked food
as i'm told everyday to obsess to back then

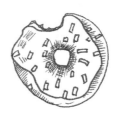

but i don't want to wear popsocks
i'd rather have tights on
i don't want to wear school clothes
i'd rather have mine on
i don't want to pretend
i know that that time's gone
and i don't really want cupcakes
i'd rather have scones
or any damn cake without fairy wings on

and with each sleep i'm getting older
only death is going to stop that
i can go with it and live

or live life looking back
i can raise my little girl to think
her meaning stops at twenty
dreams of never never land
where ticking clocks
are all the enemy
and this little girly culture
is now helping with that step

school uniform parties!
cupcakes!
botox!
tucks!
stress!

obsessed with being *so* young again
as if those days were best
as if alice stayed down that hole
and never left again

frozen in tea-party time
madhatters mice
and children's rhymes
never women!
girls for life!
lollipops and glittered icing!

for me this life is more enticing
so just in case you don't hear right
i'll say it twice again

i like living life as a woman
i'm looking forward to living life as a woman

Classic Cupcake Recipe

INGREDIENTS
110g butter softened
110g caster sugar
110g plain flour
2 tsp baking powder
$\frac{1}{4}$ tsp salt
2 medium eggs
1 tsp vanilla extract

METHOD
Preheat the oven to 180C/ 350F / Gas 4
Line a muffin tin with paper cases
Put the butter and sugar in a bowl
Beat until pale and fluffy
Sift the flour baking powder and salt into the bowl
Beat the eggs and vanilla and add to the bowl
Beat until just combined
Spoon the mixture into the paper cases
Bake for 18 to 20 minutes until risen golden and firm to the touch
Cool in the tin for 10 minutes then transfer to a wire rack to cool completely

Best enjoyed shoved in your gob or decorated with twice as much icing as anyone can handle so you can lick all the icing off the top and then eat the sponge cake bit as you would have eaten it before you put the icing on it in the first place

Alternatively – buy a cupcake from one of the five million two hundred and eighty seven thousand cupcake outlets in the UK (rough guess)

For a more adult version of the cupcake go to Paris where they are best enjoyed eaten slowly with a small espresso

S.WAINWRIGHT

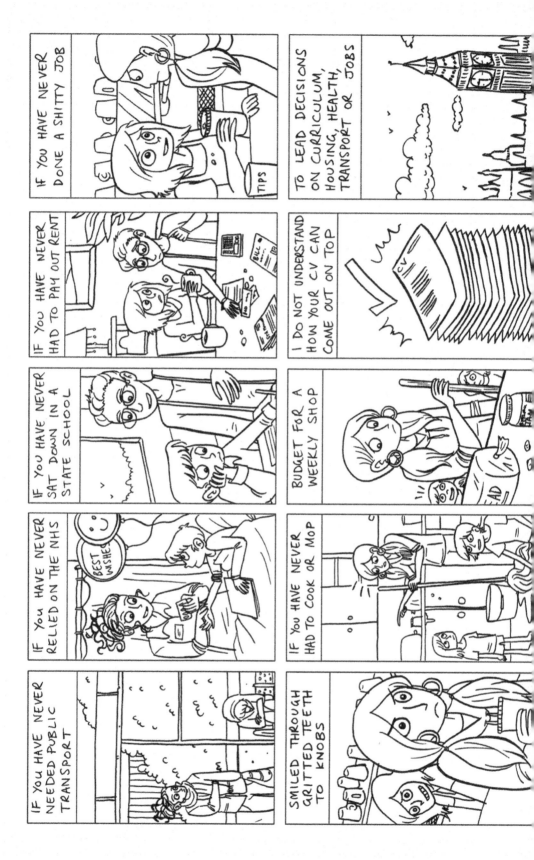

DEAR LONDON

sometimes i feel like punching you in the face
sitting directly on or bashing through your fence
sometimes i like to pretend i've never heard of you – like
who?
puzzled face – eyebrows down
hands pressed to mouth – like –
london?
where's that then?
as if i have not heard a whisper of this
london-something-place
people say is the centre of our country
south in fact
it's not as central as all that
it seems leeds is more placed for that

london
yes – i know it

the place where nights light up
where every government decision is written up
and the way rich people talk is held up by my glasgow grandmas
as the voice we should all strive for
the afternoon drama – bbc radio 4
they say the man down their street
was taught to talk like that
at public school
and now gets paid a lot

london
the place where shops don't shut
and which sometimes acts as though
outside its east – west – north and south
is a black cloud full of small unimportant towns
and villages

where people sit and dream
like hobbits driving tractors
arrive to school on horses
vote bnp and spout small town
racist thoughts
backwards

sometimes i think london thinks
everyone outside its streets walks
backwards

london
i work with you a lot
and i love our time together
you ask me to come to you
to read my poems
for gigs
in clubs
in theatres
and i know immediately from your emails
that it is you
because you do not state the place
you are the only emailer I get
that does not state a place
as if london is the default point
from which all lives relate

dear hollie – are you free to do a gig at this time on this date?
dear hollie – are you free to meet up at this time on this date?

and i love writing back to your london emails – london
to ask where that will be?
is that in manchester? i say
or glasgow maybe?
where is it?
just to remind you
not everyone lives and breathes
in just one city

london
i don't know how many times i have to tell people i'm not from you
born in reading – schooled in newbury – nights in thatcham
weekend adventures in bucklebury common
my shops aren't open late like yours

i love you london
i do
but some people here are scared of you
of your thousand theatres and underground
people sprinting round and round
your late night streets
your heaving busy city fuss
i have one bus

but london
i think you're just as scared of us

of places you have never been
of smaller towns and village greens
that did not used to be a queen's back garden

i pick blackberries on saturdays
at night there is not a sound outside my window
and i wake up to the birds
there is no youth club or southbank centre
roundhouse-spoken-word-group-poetry-slam-writing-retreat
one fish and chips a curry house three pubs
and fifty-seven trees stand on my street

perhaps one day you'd like to come and visit me
instead

there's one bus
if you're brave enough
get on it

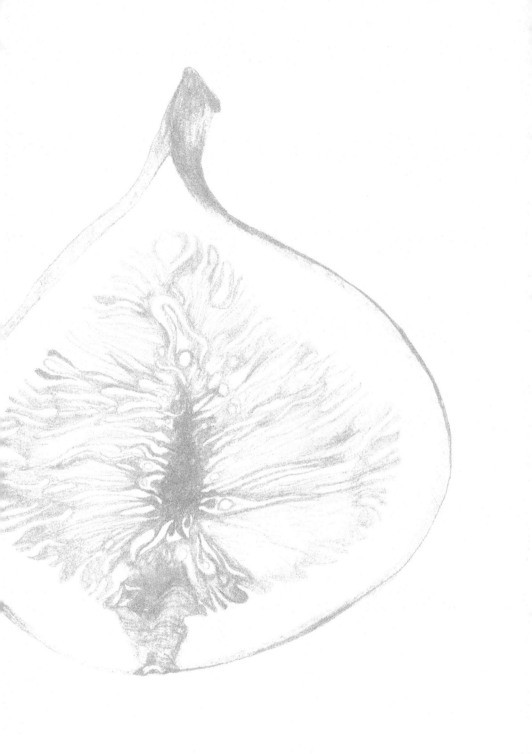

EAT MY FIG: AN INTRODUCTION

People ask me quite a lot if I'm a rapper. Or tell me that I'm like a rapper. Or tell me I should be a rapper because my poems rhyme and I read them pretty fast and they're sometimes rhythmical. But I always say no. Not because I don't like rap but because I'm not a rapper.

Rap for me is an amazing skill when done well. It takes a lot of practise and passion and a somehow superhuman ability to fit words to a beat in such a way that if you took away that rhythm, took away all the beats and all the music, the beat would still be there, strapped tightly within the words that the rapper has fitted it with. I can't do that.

The next poem has been described by some people as a criticism of rap music; of its misogyny mainly. It's not. It's a poem I wrote while watching one video by one rapper called Flo-Rida. If you haven't seen the video, it might not make sense, but basically he's lying topless on a four corner bed on a beach singing *Can you blow my whistle baby* to loads of women who are swimming in the sea. And there's a bit in a rave too. I think the song is pretty weak. I don't think rap music is in general. The poem is about the words of this song. I wrote it at my grandma's house after we talked for a while about Miley Cyrus and what an orgasm is.

So just in case you haven't seen the clip and still want to read the poem (it's pretty long because it fits in time to the music video) this may help a bit:

GLOSSARY

FLO-RIDA Rapper from the USA
BLOW MY WHISTLE Very catchy song sung by Flo-Rida
GOK WAN UK TV presenter
ZUMBA Dance fitness programme that combines latin and international music with body workout
WOMEN Extras paid to pretend they are desperate to give blow jobs to the lead singer after a quick swim

DEAD PREZ US Hiphop duo
MIND SEX Track by Dead Prez which includes the repeated lyrics *before we make love let's have some good conversation*
FIG A fruit used as a symbol in many different cultures throughout time
EAT MY FIG The female equivalent to blow my whistle (according to my friend Franny)

EAT MY FIG

I don't know about anyone else but I find this video quite strange: Flo-Rida on a bed in the middle of a beach rave. He starts off by showing us he's a really good Christian, next to a chapel on a cliff before everyone starts all this whistling. He's wearing white to show he's pure and bright, his arms wide out like Jesus Christ before he goes down and surrounds himself with some really nice women.

He is so happy because it is sunny and everything has gone to plan; there's a group of lovely looking women and he's the only one hot man. However, I wonder if he's worried that the women might be lesbians on the beach to party and pout at their gay friends. Not because of how they look or the way they move or dance but because how many straight friends do you have that go and swim and shake their ass at parties with only one guy around? One strange solitary male who has moved his bed onto the beach and sits there singing to himself? Unless he is the next Gok Wan giving them advice on the Summer season's swimsuits and how to wear them right? Then I think again. Perhaps I've got it wrong. Flo-Rida is the instructor and there's a new Zumba class going on.

I know this is just a song. I know it's only make believe. It is a very sexual fantasy and every man is allowed to dream. So Flo-Rida has a heaven where his beach has got a bed and one by one the women come along to swim then give him head and he stands before them like a God of Love, arms stretched like Christ again and there's some random blokes diving off a cliff into the sea. His friends perhaps or locals who weren't invited cos all the women fancy Flo? Who knows. Anyway, we're back to the beach and lips up close that like to blow.

And the women want to lick him because his sweat tastes so damn nice and he wishes that this perfect scene is how he lived in real life and as they dance about and everyone is feeling pretty ripe he starts to sing the chorus, the really important lines, he sings:

Can you blow my whistle baby
whistle baby, let me know

A very subtle way of saying he would really love a blow job, which brings me to the actual thing I find a little odd and that's the metaphor this man has used to talk about his knob. As he stands, shirt off, his muscles flexed in a world of his own make pretend where these women aren't all paid to dance but fancy him and call his phone and groan for him and he's the don and can film anything he wants and as the climax comes, a horse rides on, the night club chorus moves along, he sings: *Can you blow my whistle?*

A whistle. A tiny thing. I can't help but laugh. A whistle, a small and shiny thing which no-one really needs to learn because it's a pretty easy blow so I don't really think he needs to *show us girls* or *start off very slow* and it is hard, I guess, but hardly sexual, it's a tiny pocket thing mainly blown by men for men – referees or army sergeant captains – and in a fantasy of orgy raves where women go to blow his piece, at least choose a metaphor that doesn't squeak.

Can you blow my saxophone, maybe? A saxophone, a substantial thing. A saxophone takes practice and someone does need to show you how to get air in, so Flo-Rida's lines about teaching us how to do it might be sexy with a saxophone as he slowly talks us through it because there are proper mouth techniques to learn and tongue and hand positionings and when you learn to blow *that* perfectly, the tunes it starts to sing *are* sexy – blues and jazz and funk, proper music lovers' spunk that makes you want to stick your ass out and rub up on a lover's bump, to dance until the moon gets low and the next day sun is coming up, not high pitched squeaking whistles that we use when someone's just messed up or to signal something's wrong like that a footballer is off-side again. A sound that makes you want the person blowing to be quiet again.

But if everybody learnt to touch the way musicians play a saxophone; if everybody learnt to move their lips to make their lovers groan then Flo-Rida might not have an empty bed but lots of women in, really licking on his skin not just looking at him, whistling, and erotic MTV might have some better songs to sing than *Come and blow my whistle*, I'll show you how to sound it – a thing that jerks and toots the second you wrap your lips around it and makes me long for days when Dead Prez would rap about it: mind sex and sexy whispers, not a whistle taking head – songs that spoke of touch not just how to turn on creepy men.

Come and blow my whistle?
Maybe go and eat her fig first, Flo.
She'll show you how to do it.
You can start off really slow.

HATE

little jake is out on the attack. he's got a knife in his hand to go stab up
a 'black' cos his dad said that that skin colour is bad and jake never
questions his dad. his dad's been in the edl since he was thirteen, believes
everything he believes cos his grandad before him believed it like slavery
is a good thing, dark skin's all the same and those people are to blame for
everything from rising crime to tax evasion. he doesn't see any difference
between caribbean or african nations, never heard the names guadeloupe,
kenya, djibouti, zimbabwe. no patience for facts. in fact, he thinks africa's a
country not a continent, just tells his son to attack. so jake goes out seeing
black with a knife in his bag

and matt doesn't even know there's this red cross on his back, he's just
sitting in maths packing his school bag as his mate walks in, sits down and
says hey, says he's heard rumours the boy round the corner school's gay,
he's says they're all the same. he says his mum says hell, fires and flames
for benders, queers and hand bent walking perves, he says t.o.k's right, the
only thing those faggots deserve is to burn. so he grabs matt, shows him a
knife, smiles and puts it back in his bag

and ryan doesn't even know they're about to walk past, he's just sitting
at home waiting to chat to his dad. he's reading the papers about more
terrorist attacks, bombs in school bags and suicide bombers apparently
bragging about christian blood on their hands. he reads the headlines
everyday and believes everything the newspapers say. his dad says they're
all the same. his gran says all muslims should be put in jail and while he's
never read one word of the koran, just says his dad says it's the book of
those taliban gangs. so now ryan goes out to get even

and sandeep probably won't even realise the reason he's just seated outside
with his school mates eating, doesn't know his smile might be wiped out
by evening as he chats about religious attacks he's been hearing. his mate
says it always the same, says the whites think they're best and it's always the
same, says the white boys at school call him names, says his dad says white
people are always the same. no difference between russia, greece, scotland

no difference between upper, middle, working class or men or women or rich or poor or personality. just says they should settle the score. so sandeep runs back to his pad, gets a knife from his drawer and shoves it into his bag

and jake doesn't even know he's about to be had, as he takes the knife out his bag seeing the brown skin of matt, as matt catches the eye of ryan the queer and ryan gets his knife ready to settle his score with sandeep and sandeep sees the pale skin of jake.

five minutes later they stand,

jake has a knife in his back and a knife handle in his hand, blade severing the skin of matt, who stands with a firm first around a handle, screaming cos of the blade in his back, behind ryan with a blade in his back and his hand, sandeep stabbed in the back with his hand on the back of the blade in jake's back as blood, blades, generalisations and false claims lie in circles of child-old corpses still on the pavement where every day, everywhere sees the same bloody fate;

hate will ever only breed hate.

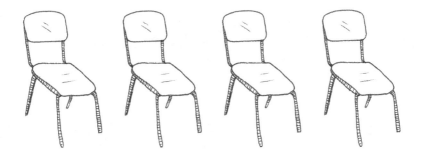

HEADACHE

if you really want to help my headache
please pass me the packet of pills
then take the pills out the packet and fill it back up
with cash notes to pay off the bills
with thrills in spas
a two-hour hot bath
with flannels
that melt down each temple's path
with low whispered voices to tickle my ears
warm sun on my shoulders
storm rain through my hair
fill it with fingers that hold my head hot
and rub me with oil in all the right spots
or just pass me the damn box
and let me get in it
lie in the dark
on my own for a minute
and chill

HUMANS

how stupid we are
in the middle of winter
up before sun
with our bodies a quiver
i wonder if animals watch as we go
struggling to work
as they peek through their tree holes
through warm piles of leaves
or cosy twig nests
saying *those humans there*
are losing their heads
the ants work all summer
to store for the frost
we work all summer
and then we don't stop
all that machinery
and still on the slog
surely less hours
or more sharing jobs
wouldn't hurt
but i'm walking to work
in this dark winter drizzle
as the animals watch me
and break into giggles

LEEK AND POTATO SOUP

This is not an experimental poem or anything, it's a recipe. Cos you're half way through the book and if this was a gig, you'd go and get a drink and go for a wee or just have a break from too much poetry. But this soup is better than that. It's my favourite recipe and the one I always make to soothe my throat after lots of gigs. I also cook it a lot while I'm practising my poems. I always cook while I'm practising my poems. Otherwise I'm just standing in my flat practising poems and boring myself with my own voice. At least this way, I have practised my poems and dinner is made for the next day already. Sometimes the flat gets cleaned too. This soup is cheap and easy. Maybe if you make it or eat it while reading the poems, they'll seem tastier – like listening to Spanish guitar while eating tapas or fish and chips with the sounds of the sea in your ears. Like in Heston Blumenthal's restaurant. This will be the same as that. Exactly the same.

INGREDIENTS
1 white onion
1 leek (white bit only or the really light almost white greeny bit but not the really green bit that is obviously green)
1 normal sized potato
1 chunk of buttered bread per person
salt and pepper

PREPARATION
Peel and chop onion
Thinly slice leek
Wash the sliced leek to get the soil out from all the layers
Peel and chop the potato into smallish bits or whatever – I like cubes

METHOD
Put chopped onion in a saucepan on a low heat with a big knob of butter (don't use margarine – it tastes crap but olive oil is ok) and pinch of salt and pepper
Stir gently on lowest heat – put lid on
Stir it around more to coat it in butter
When the onion looks mushy and see-throughish and soft – add the chopped leek – bit of salt and stir a bit more
Be patient
Imagine that you are French or Italian and that your national pride relies on slow – patient – cooking
Have a drink
Stir the leek and onions a bit more
Play Ludo with your kid if you have a kid that likes ludo
Recite some more poems to your kitchen window
Stir the stuff in the pan around a bit more while whistling
When the leek and onion looks mushy and see-throughish and soft and doesn't really smell like leek that much anymore – add the chopped potato

Stir it all round a bit more cos you think that soaks in the flavour but are not sure it is actually doing anything
Turn up the heat and add enough cold water to cover the stuff in the pan and bring to the boil
Put on the lid – turn the heat down and leave it to simmer till the potato is soft
Take it off the heat and blend it
Get a hunk of bread and spread it with a knob of butter as thick as your Aunt June used to – approx 5mm thicker than you think is healthy
Add salt and pepper to taste
Shout that dinner is ready
Add a bit more salt in panic cos you know if it tastes more salty then it'll make everyone say *this is lush, thanks Hollie – thanks mum – you're the best*
Shout again because your partner didn't hear and your daughter has her head stuck in her pirate dress costume and can't get it out
Serve with a cool glass of tap water

TOP TIP
Save a bit of the bread to wipe the dregs from the bowl – again, pretend you are cool or Italian when doing this

IF YOU HAVE KIDS
If you have a kid who says *I don't like this* (which is unlikely cos you've not fed them for the last two hours and it is lush) then say *oh, did I forget the salt?* then pretend to sprinkle salt on top – ask them if that's better – if they say no tell a hilarious story about when you used to have to eat things you didn't like when you were little and show them how by eating a raw cherry tomato which you hate – get them to count you in and watch you wince as you eat it

MARKS OUT OF TEN

i've got marks on my face to match my age
i've got a mark on my forehead where a chicken pock was scraped
i've got a mark on my shinbone from my forest biking days
you might like to take a look at them one day

i've got marks on my cheek from where I slept
i've got marks on my stomach where it shrank after it stretched
i've got marks on my breasts – the baby was well fed
i've got marks
sometimes I look at them and stress

i've got a mark on my ear where an earring used to hook
i've got a mark on my forehead from thoughtful – confused looks
i've got marks on my nails from the bites I always took
i've got marks – you can read me like a book

i've got marks on my feet from all the places that I've stood
i've got marks beside my eyes from smiles and feeling good
i've got marks around my lips from laughing till I shook

twelve marks out of ten
that's pretty good

MATHEMATICS

he says
those goddamn pakistanis and their goddamn corner shops
built a shop on every corner – took our british workers jobs
he says
those goddamn chinese and their goddamn china shops

i tell him they're from vietnam but he doesn't give a toss
i ask him what was there before that *damn japan man's shop?*
he stares at me and dreams a scene of british workers' jobs
of full-time full-employment before the goddamn boats all came
where everybody went to work for full-time full-hours every day
a british business stood there first – he claims – *before the bloody irish came*
now british people lost their jobs and bloody turkish there to blame
i ask him how he knows that fact – he says – *because it's true*
i ask him how he knows it's fact – he says – *it says it in the news*
every time a somali comes here they take a job from us
the mathematics one for one – from us to them – it just adds up
he bites his cake he sips his brew he says again he knows the plot
the goddamn caribbeans came and now good folk here don't have jobs
i ask him what was there before the *goddamn persian curtain shop*
i show him architects' plans
empty plots and closed off land
there was no goddamn shop before those pakistanis came and planned
man – i am sick of crappy mathematics
because i love a bit of sums
i spent three years into economics
and i geek out over calculus
and when i meet these paper claims

that one of every new that came
takes away *our* daily wage
i desperately want to scream
your maths is stuck-in primary
because some who come here also spend
and some who come here also lend
and some who come here also tend
to set up work which employs them
and all those balance sheets and trends
they work with numbers – not with men
and all this goddamn heated talk
ignores the trade the polish brought
ignores the men they give work to
not plumbing jobs but further too
ignores the guys they buy stock from
accountants builders on and on
and i know it's nice to have someone
to blame our lack of jobs upon
but immigration's not that plain
despite the sums inside our brains
as one for one
as him for you
as if he goes *home* they'll employ you
because sometimes one that comes makes two
and sometimes one can add three more
and sometimes two times two is much much more than four
and most times immigrants bring more than minuses

MOON

i don't look up
because i can't concentrate on my job
when i remember
i'm stood on a huge spinning planet
that waves to an orbiting rock

OCEAN FLOOR

when my daughter was three
she asked me
what was at the bottom of the sea
was it mermaids rocks and seaweed?
staring up at me
i didn't tell her the story written in the morning paper

i said
when i was her age – yes
there used to be mermaids there
gripping rocks
wishing for legs
spying on seamen on boats singing shanties
to show them the way to the safety of shores
these mermaids would splash with the turning of oars
combing their hair by the voyaging ships
dreaming of human kisses turning fish-tails to feet
playing games till night-time calls from below
when they'd go
swim away through the reefs
so i thought

i thought the ocean floor was a place for mermaids and sand
and caribbean singing crabs called sebastian
his candlesticks glowing
in ancient sea cities
through subterranean pillars
remains of palaces and titanic like leftovers on dinner plates
and parties with sea kings and octopus violinists

cynics argue – there's no space anymore – up here

now in makeshift boats
across the seas

a thousand bodies row in false beliefs
back and forth through ocean seas
from torture death or war they flee
balanced between a boarded seat and maybe
reaching safety
we say
go back – there is no space on our land

as they row on with hopeful hands
we wait
our seashores now barricaded by wires
lighthouses replaced by blue siren fires
mermaids dashed off rocks
where border control guards now sit and watch
and wait
shining floodlights of teeth into villainous waves
they wait
drowned in the soft glows of gloating
guns rested between fingers
ears pricked for shivers
they wait
for those boats
floating where black night skies above the ocean burns with cold
and frozen winds pierce fleeing souls
and never ending waves wake screaming babies
and frightened people huddle
dreams of little more than reaching safety
we say
go back – there is no space on our land

dunkirk now far from our minds
where newspaper stories
bragged of boats saving scared fleeing flesh
the worn paddles blessed
by man's compassion
our headlines now read
go back

as hands row for weeks forward and back
we say go back
as fingertips shiver and crack
we say go back
as faces think back to the homes they had
we say go back
as whispering voices break with tears
eyes full streaming freeze with fears
and just when their boats are getting near
we say
go back – there is no space for you here

here
in a land where sheep graze gracefully on never-ending rolling hills
and vodka spills from disco dancing hands
where grandmas do lunch over sandwiches
three tiered trays toppled by victoria sponges and rock cakes
and scones and jam and clotted cream
with silver spoons stirring our sugary teas
we say
go back

i watched titanic five times on the big screen
tears streaming down my cheeks as i heard the oarsman shriek
is anybody out there? is anybody still alive?
flashlights on black night skies searching for living
through freezing waters praying for shivering skins
or whistle sounds
or splashing or breathing
or anything

i used to think all flashlights in oceans were searching for bodies to save
i was wrong
with hollywood now gone
our flashlights shine in frightened faces
condemning foreign skins
we say
go back – this is our land

as desperate fathers throw blanketed children to fate
praying away from border control bullets
as babies sink into kingdoms below
where crabs dance through coral
and sea urchins blow trumpets to welcome the new crowds of visitors

as boats topple people into the party below
and corpses line seabeds with nowhere to go
and mermaids sit singing to show them the way
i hope
at least *they* say –

welcome
come here
sit down
you're safe with us now

PINK

I have never been the same
since my school teacher said
The 'sun' is a star and 'pink' is light red

PLAYING LACROSSE AT CAMBRIDGE UNIVERSITY

you said it was cute my house had a number
you said it was sweet my mum was a nurse
you said it was odd i asked the college to pay
for my match socks and tracksuit and skirt

you thought it was strange you hadn't heard of my school
you didn't know there were schools that are free
you got annoyed at all the excuses i made
not to come out for meals with the team

you thought it was great to go out for dinner and drinks
with the rugby boy blues
splash a quick quid
and you quipped and you chewed when their questions rolled in

what was it like? curious faces like an attenborough clip
what was it like? downing red wine till embarrassment chipped
what was it like?
to go to school with those state school kids?

eyes fixed on me in strangely sorrowed looks
while i gulped down the second pink bottle
as someone actually asked if it was hard to fit in *here*
with a voice that was so – *you know* – *common*

more pissed than was good i'd make excuses to wander
wondering how anyone grows up so obnoxious
by ten o'clock finding myself lost in town
phoning my friends – *i don't know where i am now*

and they'd always be waiting on call in king's college
knowing i was gonna be touchily trollied
don't go again hollie
after another of those god awful dinners

so thankful for them – the mum i could call just to vent
amelia knott – my only team friend
dad's constant help to breathe backwards from ten
they're no better than you love – we're no worse off than them

but after one year of jaw gasps and jokes
tweed jacketed blokes
old school girl networks
old school boy networks

of serious discussions in scoff-ready groups
what do people without a-levels even do?
can they spell?
oh the hoot! *hollie –*

do you mind if we don't walk together in public?
did you know we're the creme de la creme?
and though most people weren't like them at all
second year – i transferred to football

on the plus side – i can still picture my mum
oxford v cambridge – end of year one
running towards me mouth cracked in giggles
holding her grin to stop it from splitting

cos we beat oxford seconds
and someone just shouting *spiffing!*
mum's lips to my ear tearily whispering
in real life!

i guess the jokes worked from both sides

REVERSE

i would love to reverse things for one day
a short break for those who say it's all ok here
for just one day
i'd like to see what people who don't care less would say
if the media flipped
the other way around

for just one day
the women's lifestyle section of the magazine rack stands
would see a sea of choice of topics
not just diets fights and looking good
but graphics politics fashion
sport and art – food and science
top shelf porn – perhaps
and watch as we all look forlorn
and wonder why men's lifestyle sections
are full of naked pouting men on covers
fighting others in their underwear

for just one day
i swear i'd scream
to see daytime tv
presented by a bunch of grey-haired
laughter-line laden
female presenters
while the younger male side kicks giggle politely
at everything they say
while worrying how old they can get
before a younger guy
is inevitably hired instead

for just one day
i would like to see a newspaper
take a double spread about obama's arms

when *he* wears short sleeves
ten pages to talk about the prime minister's
choice of socks and hand cream
while focusing on kate middleton's degree
and how she feels about personal freedom
next to images of prince william's
top ten jackets worn this summer season

for just one day
i'd read the sports pages
and tabloid news reporting
without watching as we gawp
at twenty year old tits
as i worry about our kids growing up
in a place where family newspapers
still parade our girl teenagers' bodies
and so many deny any current inequality
and tweets threaten rape
for a female face on our money

and for just one day – i wonder what would happen

if there were airbrushed
half dressed posed men
on the front of every women's magazine
and airbrushed
half dressed posed men
on the front of every men's magazine
and airbrushed
half dressed posed men at the front
of every shop window
and loads
of fully dressed women
in photos
everywhere
cameras zoomed into their faces
in shoulder shots
their wrinkles photo-shopped deeper

like every great gq magazine man feature

for just one day
i'd have an mtv
where every other male celebrity
was dancing on a pole in pants
instruments banned
while all the females
fully clothed
stood back
just singing
or strumming away
cos that's their talent

for just one day
i'd have a grammys
where all the male performers pretend that they are strippers
as my male mates complain
is it not enough that he is an amazing singer – why can't he wear clothes
in his videos for f'sake and why does have to wear a flashing crocodile
toothed jock strap every time he performs on stage?

and i might hear friends say
why do i have to watch two men
in g strings
pretending to shag one another
in a dance routine
on x factor
at 7 o'clock in front of
my son?

and i might hear people say
*why is sex always defined as
when she comes?*

and i might hear people say
*ok
maybe you're not just on your period
maybe you're not just jealous of her tits
maybe there is more to this*

SILENCE

silence
is how i respond to shouts
is how i calm myself down
is how i let anger out
walk out from cheating men
lying friends
and funeral caskets

silence
is how i show my trust
when i sit with you in soundless words
of smiles and hugs and sleeping
is how i weep when it takes more than tears
when i cannot get my mind to work
where i hold my fear
hearing sounds that are not there
tiptoeing out of films i watched
too late at night, alone
is how i stroke your hair and hold your hand
stand beside your bed
and watch your face until you fall asleep
is how i sneak out and sneak back in again
to check on you

silence
is how i respond to bad news
and good news
and great news

silence is how i write
what i wake from each morning
and fall asleep into each night

SPIN

when i was younger
i got pissed
a lot
and snogged a lot of boys
spin the bottle was never really a surprise
when we got the hang of the
slow-pretend-to-throw-it-turn
mathematically calculating the angle perfectly to land on who we wanted

everyone of us agreed
that miles
had eaten doritos before the game
cool original flavour
the taste of each tongue was like melted cheese
we laughed for weeks about it
then let it be

when i was younger
i weed outside at parties
in farmers' fields and northcroft park
groups of girl friends forming single-sex circles in the dark
protection from childhood fears
and the boys' prying eyes
laughing through squatted bare-bummed noises
we always began in unison

when i was younger
friends stared at me confused again
as i cried compulsively at house parties
over gavin bush
and how if we got married
my name would be the
best – thing – ever

when i was younger i got pissed
with friends
who snogged the boy i fancied when i was too shy
liquid – friday night – room 2
in the loos crying
sat on the netball coach
on saturday mornings in silence
by the final whistle – always brighter
feeling slightly foolish at school on monday
but that was all
that was that
done

memories we etched and left
in the fields and houses
and toilets where they happened
embarrassing
then blurry or forgotten
kisses sticking to the lips
of the lads they were planted on
and the things done
now only to be found in old diaries or poems
or the school shirts we soaked in dirty words before gcse leave
coloured felt tip nipples
highlighting our dreams
of summer thrills

when i was at school i didn't grow up being photographed and filmed
no instagram no selfies no ipads iphones snapchat
no camera phones no digital
developing was so expensive then

involved a camera
a trip to town
and the risk of paying out six pounds
for a collection of potentially
very shit photos

sometimes the whole roll got spoilt
sometimes the stolen camera revealed twenty shots of one lad's *face*
it wasn't worth the hassle

on special occasions we did
collected them together from boots
cheap one week development
saturday trip flicking through
cringing giggling
one copy
then placed back in the envelope
in a shoe box in the cupboard in laura's room
behind the shiny two tone dress i always wanted to wear
if i'd had any boobs

no quick way to share them again
except by meeting up
and looking through them together

when i was younger
i made a prat out of myself
more times than i care to remember
memories never caught on tape
no cut and paste
no picture proof
just left to look back on
sometimes to sting a little sweet

i think it's harder growing up now
now that developing is so cheap

fishermen, the materials of which are brought from Bridport, affords employment to a portion of the inhabitants. The London and Brighton railway was constructed by a company ... act of parliament, passed in July, 18.. which they were empowered to raise a joint-stock ... 00,000, and by loan £600,000. The lin... ...d Sept. 21 1841, diverges from the Lo... railway, about 9¼ miles from Lond... ...e east of Croydon, within a short d... gate, and within 1½ mile of Cuckfield... ...mination at Church-street, Brighton... branch of 5½ miles to Shoreham, ope... Including this branch, the whole le... ...s nearly 48 miles, and the distance be... ...and the terminus at the Greenwich... The earthworks are heavy th... ...unting to 6,861,680 cubic... an elegant structu... ...by a colonnade, ab... ...wa completed in... of parliamen... Thursday, b... the inhabita... Sept. 4th; ... but has fail... was built o... The town is... trates, who... a constable,... chosen annu... The direction of poli... ...trusted, under an act of parliam... ...y of 112 commissioners, electe... ...appoint a town-clerk, survey... ...duties, police officers, &c... ...passed in 18.0, for establishing a cour... ...covery of debts under £15. By t... act of the Year of William IV., cap. 45, the town... ...a borough, consisting of the parishes of... ...and Hove, with the privilege of sending two m... ...the right of voting is vested in... ...household... the returning officer is annually... ...by the... of the county. It is a polling-pl... ...division of the county. A new to... ...on the si... of the old market-h... ...town, at an expense of £30,... ...age edifice, ornamented with thr... ...and containe offices for the magistra... ...directo... of the poor, &c., the lower part being used as a market-place.

The LIVING is a vicarage, with the rectory of West Blatchington consolidated... in the king's book at £20. 2. 1¼.; present net income, £1041 ; patron, Bishop of Chichester; impropri... J. Kent, Esq. The parish church is a spacious ancient structure, partly in the decorated, and partly... later style of English architecture, with a square embattled tower which from its situation on the summit... hill 150 feet above the level of the sea, serves as a land-mark to mariners; it contains a fine screen of... carved oak, and an antique font, said to have been brought from Normandy in the reign of William the Conqueror, which is embellished with sculptured representations of the Last Supper, and of the miracles of our Savior... is well arranged, and contains 1150... most of which...

373

are free... ...the old churchyard, a new one was co... ...pposite side of the road, leading out of... ...n 1826. The vicarage-house, ...mbent, is a handsome resi... St. ...f ease to St. Nicholas', in the north end of the town, in the ...ish architecture, with a square em... ...pinnacles, erected in 1827, at... ...raised partly by grant from the... ...oners, and containing 1840 sit... ...ee. Handsome windows of s... ...n the centre is a representa... ...Evangelists, were inserted at the expense of... ...ing is a perpetual curacy, net incom... ...Vicar.

The... ...e, is a neat plain edifice... ...00 are free. The ...£180; patron, ...ains 1000 sit... ...a perpetual ...p, Esq. The ...n the Grecian... ...and... ...ving is a ...cum... ...rge, ...ician ...tains... ...free... ...ving is a perpetua... ...and incumbent, the... ...the church of St. Marga... ...d contains 1000 sittings of which... ...g is a perpetual curac... ...ge of F. Reade, Esq. The... ...00 sittings, of which... ...al curacy, in the... ...rch, in the Mon... ...hich 624 are fr... ...patronage of... Proprietor... ...the Evangeli... ...of which 625 a... ...he... ...n the patronage of th... ...ch of St. Andrew, in Waterloo... ...in the... of Hove, contains 500 sittings... ...0 are... ...living is a perpetual curacy, i... ...rona... ...Proprietors. A new church, o... ...the fir... ...was laid in July, 1838, has been... ...d by su... ...ion, aided by a specific grant fro... ...church... ...oners; it is of the Grecian Do... ...and contains 211 sittings, 707 are... ...free... ...erected in the eastern portion... ...own, ...hich his late Majesty, William... ...contributed... ...nd her Majesty, Queen Adelaide... ...There... ...places of worship for Particula... ...ists, th... ...ndependents, and one each for th... ...iety of... ...those in the connexion of the la... ...ntess of... ...gdon, Huntingtonians, Methodist... ...Scottis... ...ers; also Bethel chapel, in connex... ...the Ma... ...riend Society, a Roman Catholic ch... ...and a sy... ...There are numerous free scho... ...principal of wh...are, the school in Gardener... ...et, for girls, founded and endowed in 1811,...

TEN ENGLISH GENTLEMEN

Ten English gentlemen sit down in the sun
Say they've nothing on these foreign folk but the land is overrun
say England was pure paradise
now they can't even enjoy a nice
scone and cream and jam or tea without hearing foreign tongues

Ten English gentlemen sipping in delight
One reads from the dictionary and tells them all a line
says that Tea is from a Chinese phrase
kia from the older days
they hit him in the face and that leaves nine.

Nine English gentlemen sitting in the sun
Say they've nothing on these foreign folk but their land is overrun
say England was pure paradise
now they can't even enjoy a nice
scone and cream or cup of kia without hearing foreign tongues

Nine English gentlemen setting scones on plates
One picks up the book again and reads out from a page
says cream comes from an Old French word
cresma's how is should be heard
they hook him to a bird and that leaves eight

Eight English gentlemen sitting in the sun
Say they've nothing on these foreign folk but their land is overrun
say England was pure paradise
now they can't even enjoy a nice
Cup of kia scone and cresma without these foreign tongues

Eight English gentlemen spread cresma made in Devon
Speaking about history and how purity is heaven
one looks round uneased
reads tea leaves really are Chinese
and jam comes from the Portuguese
they feed him to the bees and that leaves seven

Seven English gentlemen sitting in the sun
Say they've nothing on these foreign folk but they wish they wouldn't come
say England was pure paradise
now their kia breaks are not as nice
and cresma marmelada bites are interrupted by these foreign tongues.

Seven English gentlemen sitting doing tricks
One opens up the book again and sits down looking pissed
says Folk derives from folka
the Lithuanian word polka
they strap him to a boulder – that leaves six

Six English gentleman nodding heads in strife
One reads out a page again and gives them all a fright
says Paradise is Paradesh
a Persian word or Greek at best
they slap him on the head and that leaves five

Five English gentlemen sitting in the sun
Say they've nothing on these foreign polka but they wish they wouldn't come
say England was a Paradesh
now they can't even have a rest
cup of kia scone and cresma without hearing foreign tongues.

Five English gentleman stamping on the floor
One picks up the book and starts to read aloud once more
scones are Dutch
he reads – oh fuck
he ducks a punch looks up and runs and that leaves four.

Four English gentlemen sitting in the sun
Say they've nothing on these polka but their Angleland is done
say Angleland was Paradesh
now all they hear is foreignness
like goddamn déjà vu they said
like goddamn déjà vu
can't even get a cup of kia schoonbrod cresma marmelada
without hearing foreign hoots

Four angry Englishmen sit sitting on the green
Nodding heads they all agree
Rewrite British History
Invent a purebred ancestry
Ignore all factuality
And stand up for MP

//
There are several different ideas about these words' histories. The point is that they have histories outside *the UK.*

TINKERBELL

the coolest fairy on the block
her mind as sharp as grated ice
her whole being comes to life
when light glows on
a hammer

first touch and she's enamoured
glowing metal hue
the others looked on jealously
no object glowed as zealously
a tinker through and through

now she's the star of pixie hollow
high bun
short skirt
doey-eyed
slow motion introduction as the camera moves
to thighs from shoes
slightly weird shoot for a kids' cartoon
the fairy guys –wide-eyed – swoon
fairy goggles steaming up
fair enough
but the cut was made herself
with scissors hooked on acorn shelves
a shorter skirt – more practical
shoes tailored nailed
and sliced
with naked thighs and bobbled shoes
steeped in piles of screws and bolts
fascinated
by the things we drop
an old abandoned music box
that only she can mend
by cogs

by late night saws
and pulley systems
postergirl of pixie hollow
and mechanical engineer
of the entire fairy kingdom
as jaw-dropped friends
watch the dancing figure twirl again
the snow owls fly to heaven
baskets woven through those tiny tinker hands

so why are there no products to match this tinker fairy brand?

where is the tinker fairy tool box?
key and locks?
pulley toy?
the kind of stuff we'd market
if the characters were boys?
i swear to god there'd be
a lost things set
tinker toolbelt
music box to mend yourself
cogs to colour
glowing hammers
lining every tinker shelf

can you fix cogs like tinkerbell?

instead the belle has got
a million tea sets
handbags
glitter belts
and fancy dress
none of which are relevant
to her character or skills

as she sits hammering at lost things
and re-designing her next build

CoLouring Fun!

Use the picture above to colour in Tink while she
hammers away at her new invention!
What do you think she's making?
How many cogs can you see in the picture?

TOUCH

what's wrong with kissing
lips together hands caressing skin?
what's wrong with just touching
bodies together heating breathes on our...
i think we've gone too far now
can we please stop
and turn the clock a little back now?
it seems we're slipping too damn slack now
watching one type of porn
instead of hot hands
rubbing on backs now

we're sending fake-arsed facebook pokes and hugs
simulated sex and we're forgetting how to make real love
no more secret meetings under trees in springtime
just an x at the end of an msn like that's a real sign

i want to see
unbuttoned shirts to knickers
circling chests
with the tips of your fingers?
i want hands on
lips on
heat on
eyes to eyes
single biggest turn on

i want to turn off the tv cos believe me i'm not turned on
by dvds of over-greased men
on girls on
stiletto heel sofas
bent over the bed
giving head – two shouts
and no sweat – no

i want you to see me
i want you to feel me
i want to spend the day with you
sweet day dreaming
i want to hear you screaming
softly for more
not this bitch style be my whore
i'm bored of mtv thug style sessions
that's a con
i want to bring back lessons
in caressing and turn ons
make us understand the song that bodies can sing
to bring you to your knees – just tickling

i want to whisper in your ear in french
i want to breathe in your smell like a flower's first scent
je veux caresser tes hanches – t'embrasser avec langues
je veux sentir tes touches comme on peut casser le temp
je te veux sous mes hanches sans un son en silence
sipping your eyes like a sweet summertime song

i want to make you smile just speaking
tell you things make even the machoist man
weep
and if i'm tied up
you can untie those knots
shatter time for a slow wine
and a bed post stomp
so we can stop

for a minute

lie back
fill up a bath
and lie in it

under bubbles and water massaging my skin
i want to close my eyes – sigh and drift away sleeping

in my dreams
i want to remember the days
before technology tease took the real thing away

bring back breezes and seas
i want beaches and trees
i want to lie back in leaves
get my back scratched by branches
and please
bring back those basic treats
oil on your back making muscles feel sweet

i want two claps
stand up for a standing ovation
for the people still cooking up
creating temptation

i want strawberries fed to me four days a week
weak at the knees at the place where you're placing that cream

i want shaded benches
and three hour hugs
slow songs brought back
at the end of every nightclub
i want to see couples grind hard
on the dancefloor
not puking in toilets
and starting fights at closed doors

i want more than one type of porn
like kissing and touching and love
from the very day that we're born
real hippy time sixties
and make love not war
not just trends
on high street t-shirts to be worn

i want warm – not luke warm or cold

i want heated hugs
less stress
and more respect for the old
don't want millions of people alone
sitting bored on their own
not been touched for a year
just wanting one hand to hold

i want to roll back time
smash webs and texting
see people holding hands
stroking skin and listening
i just want to answer the question
i asked at the very beginning
i mean

what's wrong with kissing
lips together hands caressing skin?
what's wrong with just touching
bodies together heating breathes on our...
i think we've gone too far now
can we please stop
and turn the clock a little back now
it seems we're slipping
too damn slack now
watching one type of porn
instead of holding hands
and rubbing each others backs
now

VOICE

i lost my voice when i was six
nicked at school by english kids
my *wans* and *toos* and *threes* and *f'owirs*
not exotic anymore
red hair didn't bring it back
dye bottles searched and emptied out
trips to gran's house found some bits
but nothing big to brag about
dad's irn bru downed
tunnocks wafers chewed for better gums
potato scones buttered hot
in the hope that it would come
campsies clung in muddied feet
sodden heather, weather dreich
mum's arse-dive down from the peak
dobbie's lunch-time treats
a bit o' tablet
wi yer cup o' tea?
from sugared teeth – still
the accent wouldn't stick

i lost my voice when i was six
all i'm left with now are scottish crumbs
a few wee words to wet my tongue
dissolved in thatcham's fields
and newbury's friends
sometimes in my head
still sound like them
– mum and dad

i lost my voice when i was six
i'd love to have it back

Thank you

very much for reading this book
for finishing this book
for possibly passing it on to someone else you think might like it
if you don't fancy reading it again
for photocopying the pages illegally
and sharing them with other people
or just putting it on a bookshelf somewhere

it took me a long time to take the poems i have been writing all my life
out of my bedroom notebooks and actually read them
to some other real life people
so thanks to my lovely partner for the boot up the arse to do it
and to my mum for years of listening to poem upon poem upon poem

thanks to everyone who has smiled and come to gigs
and sent emails and hatemail
thanks to dad for the support and to family and friends
thanks to all the people who bust their asses to run poetry nights we can go to
thanks to the spoken word poetry community
one of the friendliest and most welcoming groups of people i've ever known
thanks to Maddy and Matt and Michael Pederson
thanks to all the people like
Katy Long / Phillipe Legraine / Maya Angelou / Nicholas Kristoff / Sheryl Wudunn
who have read lots of research and written books about things
that I wouldn't have understood without them

last off, i just want to say that i love poetry – some of it – not all of it mind
i love poetry in books in music in nursery rhymes
i can still remember breaking into hysterics at
nobody leave the room / everyone listen to me /
we had ten pairs of scissors / and now there's only three

i have spent my entire life scribbling silly rhymes down onto pieces of paper
writing poems in secret and stuffing them in notebooks
poems about boys at school coded in bad year 9 french
poems about velocity to help me pass my GCSE physics tests
poems about economics when I should've been writing proper lecture notes
poems for mother's day cards and parties and funerals
basically – i'm a bit obsessed with poetry
with trying to get my head around ideas in a simple way
with rhyme and rhythm and words and language
so it's nice to find other people who maybe feel a little bit the same

THE END

BRICKS

turn me on
sometimes

i don't know why
there's just something

when nobody's watching
sometimes
i rub them
the roughness is lovely
i feel a bit funny even writing this down
                                        but i love it
bricks
turn me on sometimes

when they're crumbly and old
cement-chipped and derelict
i sometimes stand dreaming
staring at building site tips
wondering if i could   break   that rubble   into
                                       little   bits
                                       in my hands
and eat it

i get the same feeling with ice

i don't know why but
the feeling of ice
turns me on sometimes

when it's left
till the end of a drink
just on the verge of water
so when i crunch the ice cubes they melt gently in my jaws
i like to eat ice when i am bored

i like to eat ice before i sleep
or after sex sometimes
when i go to bowling allies
i prefer the slush puppies
without the cherry flavouring
just the
plain pure earthy basic fresh raw disintegrating ah!
crushed up ice

thighs turn me on sometimes
guys turn me on sometimes
eyes turn me on sometimes (but it depends how they're watching me)

i like to eat ice
before i eat

when it snows
i sometimes
sneak handfuls of that
instead

eating snow
turns me on sometimes
low tones (whispered in my ear)
hot baths (when no-one else is near)
shower power water sprays (my friends say *that's a common one!*)
                    Sometimes I feel sexiest when i'm the only one around

jumper sleeves (sitting half way down a hand)
doing things (unplanned)
staring (at the sky)

the stars
turn me on sometimes

as the size of this universe blows my mind
and i need to get that energy out of my skin
when you touch me those nights

i start shivering

whistling
turns me on sometimes
singing choir tones switched up so loud I feel surrounding me like they're
music turns me on sometimes
crying turns me on sometimes
laughing turns me on sometimes
wearing high heels turns me on sometimes
wearing wellies turns me on sometimes
wearing soft silky clothes
talking with someone i don't really know
watching your throat
as you speak about something
you know really well (even if i could not care less)

my head on your cold chest
turns me on sometimes

when we're touching
and i fart accidently
and we both start to laugh hysterically
and the sexy-time moment has passed
and we were so very ready
and we joke about
how can we recapture sexy after that has happened?

that
turns me on sometimes

trusting you completely
turns me on sometimes

so does eating pizza
or any italian food to be fair
hands in my hair
and bricks
– crumbling derelict bricks

so when i flick on the tv it confuses me
as the same men and women's faces and bodies
parade the stage and sexiness is explained
the same way day after day after day

i think *that* sexiness is lame
i don't believe what you say
sexiness is way more than those bodies
boobs and holes and dicks

turn ons are all different

i like ice

and i love
big
crumbling
bricks

SPACE FOR YOU

SPACE FOR YOU

Thank you to all the brilliant illustrators in this book

Enrica Casentini – enricacasentini.com
Xueyun Feng – Xueyunfeng.tumblr.com
Jenna Thomspon – www.drawberryjam.com
Dilara Arin – www.illusian.com
Sophie Wainwright – www.sophiewainwright.co.uk
Rachel Smith – www.rachaelsmith.org
Ľubica Oslancová –www.lubicacan.com
Sonya Smith – gracieeric.tumblr.com
Lydia Nowak – inkpotillustration.com/
Rachel Blackwell – www.ethereal-earth.co.uk
Rebecca Riddle – www.facebook.com/rebeccariddleart
Emma Payne – starbrooksketchbook.tumblr.com
Ana Granado – www.behance.net/anaisabelgranado
Kate Alizadeh – katealizadeh.net
Emma Conway – emmaconway.com
Catrin Welz Stein – catrinwelzstein.blogspot.com
Rachel Orme – www.rachorme.co.uk
Sally Milligan – playfulcreativity.com
Fab Funky – www.fabfunky.com
David Evans – www.daveevansillustration.com
Aurora Cacciapuoti – www.auroracacciapuoti.com

CPSIA information can be obtained
at www.ICGtesting.com
Printed in the USA
BVOW05s0809070217
475409BV00033B/373/P